Presented to

_____

From

_____

Long Life

An Assignment from God

By Larry Hutton

Published by Force of Faith Publications
P.O. Box 822
Broken Arrow, OK 74013-0822
ISBN: 0-9747558-2-6

Original Cover Art:
    David Wirginis
Interior Design:
    Larry Hutton
Editors:
    Stephen Rankin
    Jennifer Sutton
    Andrea Spear
    Larry Hutton
    Vivian Spencer

Other References Used:

The Enhanced Strong's Lexicon. Oak Harbor, WA: Logos Research System, Inc., 1995.

Strong, James. Strong's Exhaustive Concordance of the Bible. "Hebrew and Chaldee Dictionary," "Greek Dictionary of the New Testament." Nashville: Abingdon, 1890.

Long Life

An Assignment from God

An Easy-To-Understand Teaching
About God's Will Concerning
The Length and the Quality
Of Our Lives

Larry Hutton

Contents

Acknowledgements

I thank God continually for my wife, Liz, who makes frequent sacrifices as I spend time writing for the Lord. Thank you, sweetheart, for your unwavering faithfulness as a woman of God, wife and mother.

Rachel, you're the best kid in the world! Thanks for always coming into my office and jumping onto my lap. You'll always be daddy's little girl—no matter how old you get!

I recognize that without my staff I could not do the things that God has called me to do. Steve Rankin, my left-hand man (I'm left handed ☺), will have great rewards laid up in heaven for all of his "going the extra mile" for me, my family and this ministry. Also, my *angels*, Jennifer Sutton and Andrea Spear, are truly a God-send. What a tremendous blessing it is to have such wonderful people, who have a heart for the plan of God that is being accomplished through this ministry. Thank you staff—I love you all!

Dedication

I dedicate this book to two great men of God.

The first is my Pastor, Curtis Bradford, who mentored me the first four years of my walk with the Lord, and who continues to be a great example upon which to pattern my life. Your life of godliness, steadfastness and integrity are truly an inspiration to me.

The second is Rev. Kenneth E. Hagin, who mentored me for over 20 years and built many Godly virtues into my life. His walk of love was second to none. His strong faith, uncompromising lifestyle, enduring integrity and ministerial excellence are qualities which I continue to emulate in my life.

The whole family of God, both in heaven and earth, is blessed to have these men as stalwarts for the Lord. What an honor it has been for me to be mentored by them both! For that I will be eternally grateful.

Introduction

What will your life span be on the earth? In other words, how long do you expect to live? Seventy years, eighty or ninety years? And what about your physical and mental state during those last ten or twenty years—what should you expect? Will you be confined to a wheelchair, an old folks' home or a bed? Before you answer, let me ask one more question. On what or whose information are you basing your beliefs and your answers to those questions?

The scientific and medical fields have said that the average life span for an American is between 70 and 80 years. There are also many Christians who believe that God has promised humans a maximum of 70 or 80 years, depending on His will for their lives. Yet I have known people and read about others who have lived well into their nineties, and even many who have lived beyond 100 years old. Some of them who lived that long were Christians and some of them were ungodly people. Well, if God told us we can have only seventy or eighty years, then why are many people dying before that age, and many others living far beyond that age? Is God mixed up and confused, or is it possible that He told a lie? I don't think so!

Another belief that many share is the belief that everyone dies when it's their time to die. They say that God is in total control of the span of their lives and that He has set an appointment for every person as to when, where and how they will die.

None of these beliefs are scripturally sound. I say it's time to find out the truth. In John 17:17 Jesus said that the Word of God is the truth!

Chapter 1

An Appointed Time to Die?

Is there a specific day and time assigned for us to die? We will start our search for the truth by looking at the Scriptures that have formed the beliefs of individuals who assume they have an appointed time to die. Look at Hebrews 9:27. It says, *"And as it is appointed unto men once to die, but after this the judgment."*

Let's observe how other translations reveal what this verse is saying. The New Century Version says, *"Just as everyone must die once."* The New Jerusalem Bible says, *"Since human beings die only once."* The Good News Translation says, *"Everyone must die once."* God's Word to the Nations Bible says, *"People die* once." The Message Bible says, *"Everyone has to die once."*

These translations, as well as others, reveal that this verse is not saying that we have an appointed or scheduled time to die, i.e., a specific year, month, day, hour and second that we are going to die physically. On the contrary, this verse is letting us know that every human has to die, but only *once*.

In fact, if you will read verses 24 through 28, they reveal that human beings only die once, and likewise Jesus only had to offer Himself once for the sins of the world. By reading verse 27 in context you can see that it is not referring to a specific period of time, but rather an event that will happen in the life of every human being. A good paraphrase of verse 27 would be, *Every human being must die one time, and then afterwards they will be judged.*

Now, let's look at another verse that people have used to "prove" that we all have a specific time to die. It is found in Ecclesiastes 3:1-2. It says, *"To every thing there is a season, a time to every purpose under the heaven: A time to be born, and a time to die; a time to plant, and a time to pluck up that which is planted."*

Notice verse 2 says, *"A time to be born, and a time to die;*

a time to plant, and a time to pluck up that which is planted."

These verses, written by Solomon, tell us there is a "season" when certain things are done on the earth and there is also a "time" for everything. The Hebrew definition for time does not refer to an exact moment in time but rather a period of time or a time frame.

For example, it can be used when speaking of the period of time when a woman can conceive. It can also be used when referring to the time of a meal (often referred to as "mealtime"), or the time that the sun goes down (sunset). In other words, things happen "in time." Time is perpetual; therefore, when things happen they happen during "time."

So, when people are born and when they die, those things happen during a period called "time." But, this verse is not saying that we have a specific moment that we are going to die, any more than it is saying "a time to plant" means that planting must be done at a specific second in time in order to get a harvest. We all understand that seedtime and harvest are not times designated as specific seconds of a particular date, but rather a time frame in which these things must be done. (Later in this book, we will find out what our time frame on the earth is supposed to be.) Therefore, when Solomon spoke this in Ecclesiastes he did not mean that we all have an appointed time to die. If so, then God could not have said what He said to Solomon in 1st Kings 3:14. He said, *"If you will walk in my ways, to keep my statutes and my commandments, as your father David did walk, then I will lengthen your days."*

Notice what God said. *"I will lengthen your days."* In other words, if Solomon walked in and kept the ways of God, like his father David, his days on the earth would be lengthened. But if he chose not to obey God and walk in His ways, his life would be shortened. God made it very clear that Solomon was the one who had to choose how long he would live. Since this verse shows us his days could be shorter or longer, depending on his actions, then there must not have been an appointed (specific) time for him to die.

Additionally, in Ecclesiastes 7:17, Solomon spoke something that I want you to see. It says, *"Don't be wicked or foolish for why should you die before your time?"* Now wait a minute! How could we die before our time? If we have a time to die, then how could we die before that appointment? Is it an appointment or not? It must not be. Actually, this verse simply indicates that if we are wicked or foolish we will die prematurely.

There are many more verses in the Bible that make it very clear that we do not have a specific time to die. Let's discuss some of them.

Do you remember the story of Hezekiah, and how he operated in pride, got sick and was about to die? Once he repented and got his heart right, God spoke to him and told him that He would add fifteen years to his life. (See 2nd Kings 20:6.) This story reveals that the choices Hezekiah made determined whether his life would be shorter or longer.

Another story that is worth pointing out is found in Genesis chapter 20. Abraham and Sarah had traveled to Gerar. The king there, King Abimelech, being told Abraham and Sarah were brother and sister, decided that he wanted Sarah to belong to him. After taking her from Abraham, but before he had any sexual relations with her, God warned him in a dream that she was already another man's wife. Now look at what God said in Genesis 20:7, "Now therefore restore the man his wife... and you shall live, but if you don't restore her, you and your whole family will die." So, the length of Abimelech's life was determined by the choice he made. Resisting the sin would lengthen his life; committing the sin would shorten it.

In Ezekiel 18:27-32, God told the children of Israel that if they would turn from their wickedness, they would save themselves from death. But if they did not repent, their sin would cause them to die. Also, in Proverbs 15:10, we're told that when God corrects someone who has forsaken Him, and they hate the reproof, they shall die. These verses show us that our actions have a major role in determining the length of our lives, and give further credence to the truth that we do not have a specific time to die.

Do you remember in 1st Samuel, chapters 1-4, the story of Eli the High Priest? He allowed his sons, Hophni and Phinehas, to keep sinning before the Lord even though they were priests of the Lord. In chapter 2, verse 29 God told Eli that because he permitted his sons to continue in their sinful ways, he was honoring his sons more than God. Then, in verse 33, God tells Eli the consequence of his decision "...and all the increase of your house shall die in the flower of their age." In other words, their sin caused them to die prematurely!

Chapter 2

Adding Years to Our Lives

The Scriptures we have already discussed reveal that walking close to God will cause us to live longer lives. There is some great news regarding that very thing recorded in the 91st Psalm. In that Psalm, God tells us that if we will maintain a close fellowship with Him, He will cause our life to be a long one. And, during that long life, we can experience His deliverance, aid, victory, prosperity and health, i.e., His salvation.

In the 16th verse, He uses the words *"long life."* The Hebrew word for *long* means *lengthening or prolonged*. It comes from a root word which means *to make long* and is spoken in the causative tense. That means God will *cause* our life to be long.

God doesn't want to subtract days from our lives, He wants to *add to* or *multiply* our days on the earth. When we act upon God's Word (when we do what He tells us to do) then Proverbs 3:2 says *"For length of days, long life, and peace shall they add to you."*

In Proverbs 3:16 God tells us that living longer is a benefit of wisdom. He says, *"Length of days is in her right hand."* Then Proverbs 9:11 says, *"For by me (wisdom) your days shall be multiplied, and the years of your life shall be increased."* I don't know about you, but those verses inspire me to acquire more wisdom! So, let's feed on some more Proverbs (wisdom).

Proverbs 10:27 says, *"The fear of the Lord prolongs days: but the years of the wicked shall be shortened."*

Proverbs 28:16 says, *"He that hates covetousness shall prolong his days."*

These two verses are very revealing. The first verse says that fearing God (giving honor and reverence to Him) will cause our lives to be prolonged. Being wicked (living our lives apart from God) will cause them to be shortened. The second verse says that the person who hates dishonest gain will cause his life to be lengthened. That means we had better guard our hearts with regard to money matters.

There are many more Scriptures that talk about our days on the earth being extended. At this point I'm not going to take time to elaborate on them, but I would like to list some of them for you.

Deuteronomy 4:40 *"You shall keep therefore His statutes and His commandments, which I command you this day, that it may go well with you, and with your children after you and that you may prolong your days upon the earth."*

Deuteronomy 5:33 *"You shall walk in all the ways which the Lord your God has commanded you, that you may live, that it may be well with you and that you may prolong your days."*

Deuteronomy 6:2 *"Fear the Lord... keep all his ways... that your days may be prolonged."*

Deuteronomy 11:9 says to keep the commandments *"...that you may prolong your days..."*

Deuteronomy 22:7 gives more instructions of the law and reveals the outcome of obeying it, *"...that it may be well with you, and that you may prolong your days."*

Deut. 30:19-20 tells us to choose to follow God, love Him, obey His voice and cleave to Him, *"...for He is your life and the length of your days."*

All of the above verses make it very clear that we do not have a specific time to die. Let me mention one more thing spoken of in the Bible that can alter the length of our lives—honoring your father and mother!

Ephesians 6:3 says, *"That it may be well with you and you may live long on the earth."*

Exodus 20:12 says, *"Honor your father and your mother that your days may be long on the earth."*

Deuteronomy 5:16 says, *"Honor your father and mother… that your days may be prolonged."*

Read those last three Scriptures again and notice that none of them say to honor your parents until you reach a certain age. They all tell you to honor your parents, period! Not just while you're a child, live in their house, or until they have finished paying for your schooling. The Bible says that we are to honor our parents throughout our lives. It would behoove us to pay attention to this instruction. It may be a matter of life or premature death. Selah.

God's Word proves beyond a shadow of a doubt that He has not set an appointment for us to leave this earth. In fact, all the verses we have looked at point to the truth that <u>we</u> have a major role in determining the length of our lives.

Chapter 3

How Long is "Long Life?"

Now that we have established that God has not set an appointed time for us to die, and that our lives can be lengthened, let's find out how long we can live. And, as we discuss the subject of *longevity*, I not only want to discuss the *length* of our lives but also the *quality* or *condition* of them. More specifically, we will see God's will concerning the condition of our bodies in our latter years.

We have already discovered that "our days can be prolonged," "the days of our lives multiplied" and "our years increased." Additionally, "length of days" and "long life" are promised us. So the question becomes, "How long can we expect to live? How long is *long life*?"

In Psalm 91:16 God said, *"With long life will I satisfy you."* This verse does not say we can live "however long <u>we</u> want to" until we are satisfied. It says God wants to satisfy us with *"long life."* That shows us that God does not want us to be satisfied until we have lived a *long time.* He did not say, "With short life will I satisfy you" or, "With an intermediate life will I satisfy you." He said, *"With long life."* So, we're not supposed to be satisfied until we have lived the length of time that God wills for us. Since God wants us to live a long life, then let's allow His Word to show us how long that is. Then—let's not be satisfied with anything less!

Many people have used Psalm 90:10 to establish their beliefs regarding how long they can expect to live. Let's look at it.

> **The days of our years are threescore years and ten; and if by reason of strength they be fourscore years, yet is their strength labor and sorrow; for it is soon cut off, and we fly away.**

"Threescore" means 60. So, *threescore years and ten* would be 70 years. "Fourscore" means 80. So, this verse says that 70 or 80 years will be the length of our days. Or does it? Is this verse talking about us? The casual reader might think so, but a closer study will reveal otherwise.

Notice the phrase, *"The days of our years."* One might think that the word "our" is an all-inclusive word. In other words, the verse could read "The days of *everyone's* years will be 70 or 80." If that were true, then people wouldn't be dying before the age of 70, nor would they be living beyond the age of 80. Of course, we know that is not the case. Then what does this verse mean? Let's find out. Look at the 1st verse of this chapter. It says, *"A Prayer of Moses the man of God."* This lets us know that the 90th Psalm was written by Moses. He records a prayer of his during the 40 years he spent living in the wilderness with the children of Israel.

So, when he says (in verse 10) *"the days of our years"* he's not talking about us, he's talking about the children of Israel. In fact, Moses doesn't even include himself when he says *"our."* If so, then he himself would have lived somewhere between 70 and 80 years. However, according to Deuteronomy 34:7, Moses was 120 years old when he died. Therefore, *Moses* was not included in this "70 or 80 years" and neither were we! Then who was Moses referring to in this verse? He was referring to the children of Israel. Moses was making an observation about the average length of *their* lives. Let me explain.

Do you remember how the children of Israel rebelled against God and Moses when God was trying to take them into the promised land? During their rebellion they said, *"We wish God would have let us die in Egypt or we wish God would have let us die here in this wilderness."* (Numbers 14:2 paraphrase.) Then in Numbers 14:28-29 (paraphrased) God said, *"As truly as I live, what you have spoken in my ears is going to happen to you. Everyone from 20 years of age and older who has murmured against me shall fall dead in this wilderness."* And it happened just like God said. Look at Numbers 32:13. It says, *"And the LORD'S anger was kindled against Israel, and he made them wander in the wilderness forty years, until all the generation that had done evil in the sight of the LORD was consumed."*

When you read about their wanderings you find out that their continual sinning brought many curses into their lives. These curses kept bringing death into their midst. In fact, *all of the disobedient and rebellious people died prematurely!* And that is who Moses was talking about in Psalm 90:10. However, those who believed God, including Moses, Aaron, Joshua and Caleb did not die at 70 or 80 years!

Moses was 120 years old when he died, Aaron was 123 years old when he died and Joshua was 110 years old when he died. It doesn't tell us how old Caleb was when he died, but we know that he didn't die in the wilderness. And we know that he followed the Lord fully and that the Lord brought him into the land of promise. (See Numbers 14:24.) Therefore, Caleb must have been satisfied with long life as well!

So, now we know that the "70 or 80 years" spoken of in Psalm 90 does not refer to us. It refers to the disobedient and rebellious children of Israel, not those who walked with God.

"Okay, Brother Larry, now I know that according to the Word of God we do not have a specific date to die, nor do we have to die at 70 or 80 years. But how long can we expect to live, and does God have anything to say about it?"

Yes, as a matter of fact, God has given us numerous Scriptures about the length of our lives. He has also revealed to us when old age begins, as well as the physical condition we are supposed to experience throughout our latter years. To discover these wonderful truths, let's start by looking at Genesis 6:3.

And the LORD said, My spirit shall not always strive with man, for that he also is flesh: yet his days shall be an hundred and twenty years.

Did you see that? God said 120 years! Who spoke this? The Lord! So, the Lord said that we can live at least 120 years! Or did He? If He did, it means that you 60 year olds are just now middle aged. (I can just see some of you who are reading this—you are already standing taller. ☺ And I'll bet you forty and fifty year olds won't let the youth call you old anymore!) Okay, let's discuss what God said in this 3rd verse. There are definitely different *opinions* regarding what God said.

Theories

I read different commentaries and noticed that some of them said that Genesis 6:3 does not refer to the length of a man's life.

One commentary supposed this meant how many years God gave man space to repent, or the years one could live if he strayed from God (Theory #1).

Another commentary said this was not referring to the life span of a man but of the human race (before the flood), and then proceeded to hypothesize about the number 120 (Theory #2).

Then, I also noticed that certain translations of the Bible say that God promises a *maximum* of 120 years (Theory #3).

Let's discuss these different *theories*. If 120 years is the maximum a rebellious person was promised, or the space of time that God gave man to repent, then God must have been sleeping or not paying attention when Terah lived. Terah, Abraham's father, served other gods (Joshua 24:2), yet, according to Genesis 11:32, lived until he was 205 years old. And this happened many generations *after* God spoke about the 120 years. So, I decided to flush theory #1 down the drain.

Now, what about the human race existing for 120 years—what does that mean? Some believe that the time period from Genesis 6:3 until the flood came to destroy mankind was 120 years. That would make Noah 480 years old when God made the decree in Genesis 6:3.

So, the question becomes, "Can we absolutely prove

beyond any shadow of a doubt that 120 years lapsed between Genesis 6:3 and the annihilation of mankind?" Let's see if we can.

Genesis 5:32 tells us that Noah was 500 years old when he had triplets—Shem, Ham and Japheth. (I added the triplet scenario. ☺ But it is probable.) Genesis 7:6 & 11 tell us the flood came just 2½ months after Noah turned 600 years old. So, we know the flood came approximately 100 years after Noah's sons were born.

In Genesis 6:3 God makes the 120 year decree. In the 13th verse God reveals His plan to Noah (His plan to destroy mankind). The reason is found in verses 5-6 and then verses 11-13, which reveal that God was grieved at the evil and wicked ways of mankind. So He decided to wipe them off the face of the earth.

Here's where the speculation comes in. Comparing chapter 6, verse 5, with verses 10-13, would *suggest* that a very short time transpired between the time God spoke Genesis 6:3 and then spoke to Noah about the flood.

However, it is total *speculation* on anyone's part to say how long that time period was. In fact, I'll take it a step further than that—<u>we do not know</u> how much time elapsed between Genesis 5:32 (when Noah's sons were born) and Genesis 6:13 (when God spoke to Noah). And we don't know if Genesis 6:3 was spoken between those events or before them.

Verse 1 of chapter 6 starts with "And it came to pass." Since the Bible was not written in chapter and verse then God could have been tying verse 32 of chapter 5 to verse 1 of chapter 6. Since "it came to pass" is after verse 32, God could have spoken Genesis 6:3 *after* Noah's sons were born. That would mean that it was less than 100 years from Genesis 6:3 until the flood.

There is something else we need to consider here that could have an effect on this discussion. There is no way to *prove* how long it took Noah to build the ark. We have all *thought* it was 100 years. But let's think again. When God spoke to Noah about building the ark (Genesis 6:13-21) Noah's sons already had wives. That could mean that his sons were in their 30's or older when God told Noah to build the ark. So, the ark may have taken 70 years or less to build. If so, it's possible that Genesis 6:3 was spoken from 50 to 80 years before the flood!

When we use the words "it's possible" or, "we do not know" or, "God could have" we are presenting a hypothesis. We may not want to call it an opinion or theory but when we are speculating, supposing, guessing, suggesting or assuming in order to reach a conclusion, it's the same thing.

In other words, yes, it is *possible* that Noah was 480 years old when God spoke Genesis 6:3. But it is also *possible* that Noah was 500, 510 or 520 years old when God spoke it. Those who believe the "500" would have <u>just as much Scripture</u> to support their point as those who believe "480" would have to support theirs. And only a person full of pride would say, "Well, I know I'm right."

Listen, it's okay to "think" we're right. Everyone is entitled to his own opinion. But, in this case, if we say *what we believe* is "the truth" we just entered into ERROR!

Now, let's come up the other side of the mountain. Let's *suppose* that it was 120 years from the time God spoke Genesis 6:3 until the flood. Does that mean that we can say, with <u>absolute certainty</u>, God *could not* mean anything else by that verse? <u>Or, are there verses in the Bible that have double meanings?</u> Of course, any student of the Word knows there are numerous Scriptures with double references. It has been called "the law of double reference." However,

I've noticed that when a Scripture has a double reference, there are other Scriptures to substantiate the second reference.

If 120 years passed between Genesis 6:3 and the flood, then the law of double reference applies here. I believe that with careful consideration and the use of many Scriptures we can substantiate that Genesis 6:3 definitely had something to do with altering the length of men's lives.

First of all, after God spoke Genesis 6:3, and beginning with the first generation after the flood, there was a MAJOR decline in the age to which men lived. Since God destroyed the wicked on the earth, and spared righteous Noah and his family, then why didn't Noah's sons live over 900 years like men did before the flood? Noah's son, Shem, and grandson, Arphaxad, lived 350 years less and 512 years less, respectively, than did Noah. That's just two generations after Noah! Plus, if God's statement in Genesis 6:3 had nothing to do with how long human beings could live, then we need to know not only what started the rapid decline, but also what stopped it. A close study shows that around the time of Joseph, Levi and Moses, the length of man's life leveled off in the 130's.

"Well, Brother Larry, I think it was the sin and wickedness that caused the decline in man's years."

Okay, then let me ask you a question. If wickedness and sin were the cause of the sudden and continual drop in ages (from 950 years to 130 years), then why did the decline stop? Sin continued to get worse, didn't it? Why didn't ages continue to drop to 90, 60, 30, 15...?

Is it possible that God had decreed something that set a time frame, so that the impact of sin could not run its full course before the Messiah came? If you'll study it out you'll discover that God always spoke things to create or change something. And there is no reference other than Genesis 6:3 that would affect how long a man could live.

Furthermore, if sin caused the length of man's life to decline, then why hasn't the length of man's life increased the last two thousand years since Jesus defeated sin? In 2,000 years, shouldn't we be back up to living 950 years like Noah did? If sin could cause a decrease in ages (a decrease of over 800 years) in just a few generations, then why couldn't righteousness through Christ cause an increase in ages in many generations (over 2,000 years)?

It's quite evident that Genesis 6:3 *did* have an effect on how long human beings could live. Now let's dissect Genesis 6:3 so we don't have to theorize or just have an opinion. And let's use the two primary rules of Bible interpretation. Number one: read the verse in context. And number two: interpret what is said in light of other Scripture.

In this verse, God said, *"His days shall be 120 years."* The Hebrew word used for "days" is **yom**. It can be translated literally as a day (from one sunset to the next), or figuratively as a space of time defined by an associated term like the word "age." Either way, it can be defined as the length of a man's life, whether his "age" or the "days" that he lives. In fact, this Hebrew word is used in Genesis 18:11 when it says that Abraham and Sarah were *"well stricken in age."* The same Hebrew word is used in Genesis 47:28 where it tells us that the whole *"age"* of Jacob was 147 years. Joshua 23:1 uses the same word when referring to Joshua being old and *"stricken in age."* So, it is very clear that God is speaking of age when using the word "days" in this verse.

Furthermore, here in Genesis 6:3, the word "days" is used in context with the word "years." The Hebrew word for "years" is the same word used when informing us about how long certain people lived, such as Noah, Abraham, Moses, Aaron, Joshua and many others. Additionally, in this verse God speaks about man and says, *"…he is flesh, yet his days shall be 120 years."* So, *in context* God said that man was "flesh" and then proceeded to talk about the longevity of that physical body.

Listen, this verse is straightforward, plain and clear. Why should we try to "theorize" or "make up" some meaning that is not only confusing but simply can not be substantiated. (Note: Isn't it funny how we'll take the "70 or 80 years" in Psalms to mean age, but the "120 years" in Genesis to mean something else?) So, I am not going to flush theory #2 down the drain (the belief that it was "120 years" until the flood came) but neither can I establish doctrinal truth on suppositions or opinions. If you can't prove something by using God's Word, it's not for me.

Now, what about the translations that read "man's days will be *no longer* than 120 years?" If that is what God meant, then once again He must have had some mental lapses, because we have many Biblical records of men living beyond 120 years. So, I can't go along with any of those translations either—goodbye theory #3.

Now let's take an even closer look at Genesis 6:3.

Chapter 5 lists the lineage from Adam to Noah. Those listed lived from 777 years to 969 years, except for Enoch, who was translated at the age of 365. Chapter 6 begins by telling us that mankind began to reproduce rapidly, but so did their sins. Then verses 5-7 reveal that God was grieved and proposed to put an end to all living things, man and beast.

God's statement about the 120 years came during the multiplication of the sins and wickedness of man. Obviously, God decided during that time that He didn't want to put up with their wickedness for nearly a millennium (man was living well over 900 years at that time). So, God spoke and made a promise to mankind that he could live *at least 120 years*. Did I catch your attention with that statement? I hope so, because now we are going to interpret Genesis 6:3 in light of other Scripture.

Many generations after God made the statement about the 120 years, we see men of God living *longer* than 120. In fact, I will begin with Abraham (who lived eleven generations after Genesis 6:3) and give you a brief list of the names of some individuals and how long they lived, as recorded in the Bible.

Abraham – 175, Sarah – 127, Isaac – 180, Jacob – 147, Joseph – 110, Levi – 137, Moses – 120, Joshua – 110,

Aaron – 123 and Jehoiada, the Chief Priest – 130. The time from Abraham to Jehoiada was 22 generations. Jehoiada lived 130 years—and this took place over 1200 years after Genesis 6:3! Joseph and Joshua, who lived until they were 110, were the only ones listed who lived less than 120 years. Moses was the only one listed who lived exactly 120 years. Everyone else listed lived 130 years or longer.

So, what about the statement that God made in Genesis 6:3 regarding the 120 years? Do you think God got mixed up or told a lie? Of course not. Then He must not have been giving a *maximum* or an *exact* time period. He must have been giving a promise to man that he could live *at least* 120 years. However, along with that promise, there must have been a limitation placed on his life as well. That's evident by the fact that man no longer lived the 900+ years like he had before God made that statement. After God spoke "120 years," the length of man's life began declining rapidly until it leveled off in the mid to lower 100's.

The list on the following page reveals how the years of man's life started declining after God decreed the 120 years. Listed are the names of each person and the ages at which they died.

Adam	–	930 years old
Seth	–	912 years old
Enos	–	905 years old
Cainan	–	910 years old
Mahalaleel	–	895 years old
Jared	–	962 years old
Enoch	–	365 years old (translated)
Methuselah	–	969 years old
Lamech	–	777 years old
Noah	–	950 years old
Shem	–	600 years old
Arphaxad	–	438 years old
Salah	–	433 years old
Eber	–	464 years old
Peleg	–	239 years old
Reu	–	239 years old
Serug	–	230 years old
Nahor	–	148 years old
Terah	–	205 years old
Abraham	–	175 years old
Isaac	–	180 years old
Jacob	–	147 years old
Joseph	–	110 years old
Levi	–	137 years old
Moses	–	120 years old
Jehoiada	–	130 years old

Just think, before God spoke about the "120 years" in Genesis 6:3, you were not considered old until you had lived for centuries!

Now, notice that Noah was the last human being listed who lived over nine centuries. But it was during Noah's lifetime when God decreed the *120 year promise*. By looking at the list, you can see that the length of man's life started declining rapidly with the generation after Noah. In fact, 350 years were subtracted from the life of man starting with Noah's son, Shem. Then, as you scroll down the list, the length of man's life continues to decline until it levels off at around 130 years. (Jehoiada is the last person listed. He lived eight generations after David and twenty-two generations after Abraham. I point this out because a close study reveals that man's years quit declining around the time of Moses.)

Hopefully, you are beginning to see that when God speaks of satisfying us with long life, He is speaking of well over a century!

Chapter

4

Our Old Age Years

"Well, Brother Larry, it looks as though God wants us to live beyond 120 years. Why then aren't Christians living that long?"

According to all the verses we previously read, there are things that *we* can do to either lengthen or shorten our lives. And guess what? If we don't know it is God's will for us to live at least 120 years, we sure won't have the faith to embrace it. And, in light of Hosea 4:6, that could be a major reason why God's children don't live the length of time that He has promised them. If they don't know it, how could they believe for it? Later in this book, we will look at other reasons why people don't experience God's promise of "long life."

Now, let's continue our study on longevity, and discover exactly when a person enters *old age.*

When Are We Considered "Old?"

Let's discuss what *God* calls "old." However, I'm going to tell you in advance, you might have to change what you think and believe. You might have to make a decision whether you are going to believe what you read in God's Word, or what you have previously thought or been taught. I would strongly encourage you to *"let God be true"* (Romans 3:4). It definitely will have an effect on your future!

Are you ready? Okay, here we go…

The first place God mentions "old age" in the Bible is found in Genesis 15:15. In that verse, God told Abraham that he would die *"in a good old age."* In Genesis 21:2, when Abraham was 100 years old, God said he had Isaac in an *"old age."* Then in Genesis 25:8, when referring to the death of Abraham at 175 years, it says he *"died in a good old age… full of years."* (Here's an interesting thought: At 100 years it was called "old age," and at 175 years it was called "good" old age.)

Genesis 35:29 speaks about the death of Isaac at 180 years, and says he was *"old and full of days."* Notice, Abraham was *"full of years"* and Isaac was *"full of days,"* and both of them lived way beyond 120 years.

In Genesis 37:3 it says that *"Israel (Jacob) loved Joseph... because he was the son of his old age."* By reading and studying from Genesis 41:46 through chapter 47, verse 9, we can establish that Jacob was between 90 and 91 years old when Joseph was born. *This is the youngest age mentioned in the Bible that is referred to as being "old."* So, scripturally, we don't enter into "old age" until we hit 90!

However, there is a Scripture that might seem to contradict the above statement. It is found in 2nd Samuel 19:32. Let's look at it. It says that *"Barzillai was a very aged <u>man</u>, fourscore years old."* This verse appears to say that the age of 80 is very old. But many Bible translations have wrongly translated the word "man" in this verse. The Hebrew word used here is **shâmoniym.** It does not mean *man* at all. In fact, the next word found in this verse (fourscore) is the same Hebrew word. It means *eighty.* So, what this verse is really saying is "Barzillai was a very old 80 years old." You can see that truth revealed if you go on reading through verse 37. In those verses, Barzillai declares that he doesn't have long to live and that he can no longer see, hear or taste. If you saw someone like Barzillai today, you might say, "That guy looks a whole lot older than he actually is." Well, that's not the kind of physical condition that God wants us to be in at any age! Therefore, Barzillai is not an example for us to follow regarding the length or quality of our lives in our latter years. (We'll discuss that in more detail later in this book.)

So, now we know that we don't enter old age until we hit 90, and that we can still live an abundant life from that age until we die—decades later!

I told you that you might have to change your thinking and believing, didn't I?

Someone may say, "Well, I think I'll be satisfied by the time I hit 90. That will be long enough for me to live." That may be the way you feel right now, but there are two things that could change your mind. First of all, finding out how God views old age, and secondly, discovering how long He wants *you* to live. If it's *God's will* for you to live longer than 90 years, don't you want *His will* accomplished in your life?

You see, when God speaks of old age, He is not referring to someone who is crippled, sick, worn out and unable to get around. That may be the world's idea of old age, but it's not God's! Remember, Moses did more for God in the last 40 years of his life than he had during the previous 80! That's right! From the age of 80 until he was 120 years old, Moses lived a very active and physically demanding lifestyle. He led millions of people out of Egyptian bondage into the wilderness. He traveled days without water or food, he climbed Mount Sinai and received the commandments on tablets of stone, and he oversaw the entire building project when God told him to build the tabernacle

He also led a rebellious people through a tough land for 40 years. He withstood plagues of fiery serpents and earthquakes, he fought in battles and wars and defeated his enemies, and he ruled over many cities that the children of Israel had taken from their enemies. *And he did all of that after he was 80 years old!* That's because he wasn't "old" yet! He didn't enter old age until he turned 90, and even then he was still healthy and strong, with good eyesight until he died (see Deuteronomy 34:7). And right before he died, at 120, he climbed yet another mountain!

It Doesn't Pay to Disobey

Now, what I'm about to say may shock you, but I'll

prove it by God's Word. The only reason Moses died at 120, and Aaron at 123, is because they disobeyed God! That's right—they would have lived longer and gone into the "Promised Land" if they had obeyed God.

Okay, now that I've got your curiosity up, it's time for—the rest of the story! Let's read Numbers 20:7-12.

> **And the LORD spoke to Moses, saying, ⁸Take the rod, and gather the assembly together, you and Aaron your brother, and speak to the rock before their eyes; and it shall give forth its water, and you shall bring forth to them water out of the rock: so you shall give the congregation and their beasts drink. ⁹And Moses took the rod from before the LORD, as he commanded him. ¹⁰And Moses and Aaron gathered the congregation together before the rock, and he said unto them, Hear now, you rebels; must we fetch you water out of this rock? ¹¹And Moses lifted up his hand, and with his rod he smote the rock twice: and the water came out abundantly, and the congregation drank, and their beasts also. ¹²And the LORD spoke to Moses and Aaron, Because you believed me not, to sanctify me in the**

> **eyes of the children of Israel, therefore
> you shall not bring this congregation
> into the land which I have given them.**

God did not tell Moses and Aaron to "strike" the
rock, He told them to "speak to" the rock. As a result,
God told them in verse 12, *"Because you believed me
not... you shall not bring this congregation into the land
which I have given them."*

Now, let's see what happened to both of them. First,
look at Numbers 20:23-24 & 28.

> **The Lord spoke to Moses and Aaron...
> saying, [24]Aaron shall be gathered unto
> his people: for he shall not enter into
> the land which I have given unto the
> children of Israel, <u>because you rebelled</u>
> <u>against my word</u> at the water of Meribah.
> [28]...and Aaron died there in the top of the
> mount** (Hor).

In this passage God tells Moses and Aaron why they
are going to die instead of entering into the land of
Canaan. He said, *"Because you rebelled against my
Word."* As a result, Aaron died at mount Hor. Now
look at Deuteronomy 32:48-52.

And the LORD spoke to Moses... saying, [49]Get thee up into this mountain Abarim, unto mount Nebo, which is in the land of Moab, that is over against Jericho; and behold the land of Canaan, which I give unto the children of Israel for a possession: [50]And die in the mount where you go up, and be gathered unto your people; as Aaron your brother died in mount Hor, and was gathered unto his people: [51]<u>Because you trespassed against me</u> among the children of Israel at the waters of Meribah-Kadesh, in the wilderness of Zin; because you sanctified me not in the midst of the children of Israel. [52]Yet you shall see the land before you; but you shall not go thither unto the land which I give the children of Israel.

Notice, in this passage God allowed Moses to view the land of Canaan from a distance but not enter into it. Then He tells him why, *"Because you trespassed against me."* So, both Moses and Aaron died prematurely because of disobedience. But, flip that coin over for a moment—if they had obeyed God, they would have entered into the land of Canaan and lived longer than 120 and 123 years respectively. That proves to us beyond a shadow of a doubt that the "120 years" that God spoke of in Genesis 6:3 was not a maximum life span. Aaron had already passed that age, and both of them could have lived longer!

One last note of proof that Moses could have lived longer is found in Exodus 6. In this chapter, God gave the specific ages of three men of God who lived during Moses' lifetime. Verse 16 says, *"the years of the life of Levi were 137 years."* Verse 18 says, *"the years of the life of Kohath were 133 years."* Verse 20 says, *"the years of the life of Amram were 137 years."* Notice the ages of the three men listed—137, 133 & 137. Since God is no respecter of persons, then Moses and Aaron could have lived as long as these men did, had they obeyed God.

Chapter 5

Old, Yet Strong and Healthy

Even though Moses died prematurely, he was still physically fit, strong and healthy at 120! But Moses isn't the only godly example of someone being old, yet healthy and strong. Jacob was in good health at 130 years old.

You'll discover that truth in the story of Joseph when he was ruling the land of Egypt for Pharaoh. Joseph was about 39 years old when his brothers came to him and bowed down before him. In Genesis 43:28 Judah and his brothers are standing before Joseph, answering Joseph's question about their father Jacob. They answered and said, *"Your servant our father is in good health, he is yet alive."* Jacob was 130 years old at that time and they said he was in good health! Then

Jacob lived another 17 years and died at the ripe old age of 147! (Like I said, God's picture of old age is quite different than what ours has been. And all these verses we are looking at are adding further credence to the truth that we can live *at least* 120 years—in good health!)

Let's look at the life of a man by the name of Job. In the past, I've heard people ask the question "What about Job?" And in every case they were referring to Job's trials. But most theologians agree that His trials lasted less than one year! So, let's focus on the 99% of his life that was good and not the 1% that was bad. In fact, we're going to see that Job's life is a good example with regard to "long life" as well as "abundant life"—God wants us to have both!

Job 1:1 tells us that he was a man who was honest, totally devoted to God and one who avoided evil. Verse 2 tells us that Job had seven sons and three daughters. The sons' ages are not given, but verse 4 says that they all had their own houses. This would indicate to us that they were at least in their 30's if not older. Then verse 3 tells us that Job had 7,000 sheep, 3,000 camels, 500 oxen and 500 donkeys. It also tells us that he had a very great household, meaning that he had a large staff such as butlers, maids, shepherds, cooks and other employees who worked for him, taking care of all of his businesses. After all, rich men usually have many employees. And, according to verse 3, Job was the richest and most influential man of the east.

We don't know how old Job was at this point but we can guess quite accurately as to what his *minimum* age might have been. Since his sons were at least in their 30's, and since it probably took him many years to build his businesses and his wealth to the point that he surpassed all the other rich people around him, then he was at least in his 50's or 60's. By looking at Genesis 5 and Genesis 11 we can see that the youngest age mentioned for someone having children was 29 years old (that was Abraham's Grandfather, Nahor. See Genesis 11:24). So, using that minimum age, that would have put Job in his late 50's (and that is probably an extremely low guess).

Now, let's look at the 42nd chapter of Job. After Job was healed, God blessed him with seven more sons and three more daughters. That would take a few years to accomplish wouldn't it? Then, after he had his sons and daughters, verse 16 tells us that he lived another 140 years. That would put him between 170 and 190 years before he died. And we know he was healthy because God healed him and blessed his latter

years more than his former. In fact, not only was he
healthy all of those latter years, but God increased
Job financially to the point that he had 14,000 sheep,
6,000 camels, 1,000 oxen and 1,000 donkeys. You've
got to be healthy to run all of those kinds of thriving
businesses! Now look at verse 17. It says that when
Job died, he was *"old and full of days."* We know one
thing for sure. Job lived approximately 160 years (or
more) and he was healthy and wealthy all but one of
them! Glory!

Another Scripture that reveals the intended condition
of our physical bodies in our latter years is found in
Joshua 14:6-14. Caleb is the one who is speaking in
these verses. In verse 7 he said he was 40 years old
when he spied out the land. Now look at what he
said 45 years later, in verses 10-11.

> **"And now, behold, the LORD has kept
> me alive, as he said, these forty and
> five years, even since the LORD spoke
> this word unto Moses... and now, lo, I
> am this day fourscore and five [85]
> years old. ¹¹As yet I am as strong this
> day as I was in the day that Moses sent
> me: as my strength was then, even so
> is my strength now, for war, both to go
> out, and to come in."**

Wow! Caleb said he was 85 years old and just as strong physically as when he was 40! He said that he could go to war with the same strength he had at the age of 40! And it must have been true because the next few verses tell us that he asked for Mount Hebron for his inheritance and then went and possessed it. Glory to God!

I'm reminded of something that God said to us in Psalm 92:14 *"...they* [the righteous] *shall bring forth fruit in old age. They shall be fat and flourishing."*

In essence, the Hebrew words used for *fat* and *flourishing* mean that we are supposed to be vigorous, fresh and green (like a young plant). And notice, it says, "in" old age, not "until" old age. So, when we are old and "in" our latter years we are supposed to be strong physically—full of vim, vigor and vitality!

Old, With a Full Head of Hair

God even said we can have a head full of grey hair in our old-age years. Let me give you three Scriptures for that.

Proverbs 20:29 says, *"The glory of young men is their strength: and the beauty of old men is the gray head."*

I like that. It doesn't say the beauty of old men is the "bald" head, it says "gray" head. That means we can believe God for a full head of thick, healthy, gray hair when we are old—that's 90 years and up!

Proverbs 16:31 says, *"The hoary head is a crown of glory, if it be found in the way of righteousness."* I like the Good News Translation. It says, *"Long life is the reward of the righteous; grey hair is a glorious crown."*

One of my favorites is found in Isaiah 46:4. Let me quote it from the New International Version. *"Even to your old age and gray hairs I am he, I am he who will sustain you. I have made you and I will carry you; I will sustain you and I will rescue you."*

Isn't that great?! God said He would carry and sustain us even when we are old and gray-headed. God is faithful!

I trust that you are beginning to get revelation of God's viewpoint of old age. It is this: we are supposed to enjoy life *more* in the latter part of our lives than we did at the first. In our "old age" years we should be healthy, be strong physically, and have more understanding, more wisdom, more money and more possessions than we did in our earlier years. That sounds like something to look forward to!

Think about it—if you know that you can live at least 120 years and be healthy, wealthy, wise, full of peace and joy, and show God's love to everyone you meet—you'll want to live a long life on the earth!☺

Chapter 6

Full of Days

Notice again what God said in that 17th verse of Job 42. *"So, Job died being old and full of days."* Let's study out the passages in the Bible that use the phrase "full of days" or "full of years." Here in Job 42:16-17 we see that "full of days" was at least 160 years and probably more. And during all but one of those years Job had a strong and healthy body.

Now look at Genesis 25:7-8. Verse 7 says Abraham lived 175 years. Then verse 8 says Abraham gave up the ghost and *"died in a good old age, an old man, and full of years; and was gathered to his people."* Abraham, who lived many generations after God's promise of at least 120 years, fulfilled the 120 and then lived until he was "full of years." So, "full of years" in this case was 175 years. And remember, it wasn't just called *old age* — it was called a *"good old age."*

Okay, our next reference is found in Genesis 35:28-29. Verse 28 tells us that the length of Isaac's life was 180 years. Then verse 29 says that Isaac died *"being old and full of days: and his sons Esau and Jacob buried him."* Isaac, who lived many generations after God's promise of at least 120 years, fulfilled the 120 and then lived until he was "full of days." So, "full of days" in this case was 180 years.

Now let's look at 2nd Chronicles 24:15. It says that Jehoiada (the chief priest of Judah) grew old and was *"full of days when he died."* Then it says he was a *"hundred and thirty years old when he died."* Jehoiada, who lived many generations after God's promise of at least 120 years, fulfilled the 120 and then lived until he was "full of days." So, "full of days" in this case was 130 years.

> **This is the youngest age recorded in the Bible when referring to someone who was old and "full of days."**

It's also interesting to note here that Jehoiada lived eight generations after David, who lived fourteen generations after Abraham. So, we are talking about people who lived in a whole different era than the time of Noah, which is when God gave the 120 year promise.

Speaking of David, the Scripture indicates that he must have lived a long life as well. It is recorded in 1st Chronicles 29:28 that David died *"in a good old age, full of days, riches and honor."* We are not told how old David was when he died, but this verse does give us some obvious clues. First of all, it uses the phrase "full of days." If we allow the Bible to interpret that phrase we can get a *range* of how old he was. You see, many generations before David, Isaac was "full of days" and lived until he was 180. And many generations after David, Jehoiada was "full of days" and lived until he was 130. Secondly, this verse says that David died in a "good old age." The only other person referred to when listing their age and using that phrase, is Abraham. He died at 175. So, that means that David was somewhere between 130 years old and 180 years old when he died.

By looking at all the Scriptures we've studied so far, we can see that God's best for "long life" would be to reach a "good old age, full of days and full of years." Remember, old age doesn't begin until the age of 90, and it doesn't refer to one who is weak, sick and frail. So, when God says He wants to satisfy us with long life, He means that He wants us to live until we are at least 120 years old. And He wants us to be healthy and strong from 90 years and upward until we die! Now friends—*that is good news!*

"But Brother Larry, there were great men of God who died before 120. Joseph died at 110 and so did Joshua. And there have been those in our modern era who have lived far short of 120 as well. Did they miss out on God's best?"

Before I answer that question, let me say something. It would be very easy for us to ponder the above question, and then form our beliefs based on the convictions or experiences of others. And if we're not careful we can allow our emotions or even religious ideas to establish our doctrine, rather than letting God's Word determine what our beliefs should be. My mentors always taught me to establish doctrinal truth on the Word of God alone—never on our convictions or the experiences of others.

> *Doctrinal truth must be established*
> *exclusively by the Word of God.*

I was also taught to "let the Word of God speak where it speaks and be silent where it is silent." So, as far as Joseph and Joshua are concerned, the

Scripture doesn't tell us why they died. Therefore, since we have already established Bible doctrine showing us that we can live at least 120 years, then Joseph and Joshua *could have* lived longer. And since the Bible is silent as to the reason why they didn't live longer, then we have to accept the fact that we won't know the answer until we get to heaven.

However, we also have to allow the Bible to speak where it speaks, such as all the other cases of people who died after 120 and fulfilled the "120 year promise" from God. Nevertheless, let's remember that Joshua and Joseph didn't die at 70 or 80 years. They lived until they where 110 years old—and that's only 10 years short of the 120. So, they were both centenarians!

Now let's look at Judges 8:32. It tells us that Gideon *"died in a good old age."* Once again, the Scripture doesn't tell us *specifically* how old Gideon was when he died. But it is very specific in that he didn't just die at an "old age." It says, *"good old age"* placing him in the same class along with Abraham, David and Jehoiada—that being 130 years and upward.

Chapter 7

Hindrances to Long Life

In chapter 1 of this book, we looked at Scriptures about Hezekiah, Abimelech and Eli, and discovered some reasons why our days on the earth could be shortened. Hezekiah was operating in pride and it almost cost him his life. Abimelech had to resist sin or his life would have been shortened. And Eli disobeyed God and it cost him the lives of his sons!

Now look at Proverbs 15:10. It tells us that if we hate correction it will kill us! On the other hand, if we listen to God's chastisement (correction) we will live long on the earth! How does God correct us? With His Word! It is sharper than any two-edged sword and will cut away the wood, hay and stubble in our lives. The Word shines the Light on our pathway, showing us places in our lives where we are missing it. This gives us the opportunity to change our ways and thereby extend the length of our days. Hallelujah!

Proverbs 3:1 tells us to fill our minds and hearts with God's Word and then live by it. When we obey verse 1, then verse 2 says, *"For length of days, long life, and peace shall they add to you."* But the opposite would also be true. If we choose to disobey what God's Word says, then *reduced days, a short life and turmoil will be given to you.*

It would be wise of us to adhere to this "wisdom" in Proverbs. God wants us to know that His wisdom will cause us to live longer. Proverbs 3:13-25 speaks of the benefits of walking in the wisdom of God. Verse 16 says, *"Length of days is in her right hand."* We could say it this way, "Long life is in her right hand."

Proverbs 9:11 also speaks of the benefits of wisdom, *"For by me your days shall be multiplied, and the years of your life shall be increased."*

"That's wonderful, Brother Larry, but how do I get this wisdom?"

Look at 1st Corinthians 1:30. It tells us that if we are *in Christ* then all of God's wisdom is in us and available to us. First Corinthians chapter 2 tells us that the Holy Ghost, who lives on the inside of us, will teach us God's wisdom. Colossians 2:3 tells us that in Christ (that's where we are) *"are hid all the treasures of wisdom and knowledge."* Then Colossians 3:16 tells us that all wisdom is found in the *"Word of Christ."* And finally, James 1:5-6 tells us that if we need wisdom for any situation that we are facing, we can ask God for it, receive it by faith and He will give us more than enough!

Now let's look at a couple more Proverbs regarding the shortening or lengthening of our days. Proverbs 10:27 says, *"The fear of the Lord prolongs days: but the years of the wicked shall be shortened."* Notice, the years of the wicked shall be shortened. The word *wicked* refers to someone who is against God. Simply put, it means someone who doesn't believe in Him. But the first part of the verse tells us that if we revere and respect God then our days will be prolonged.

A similar verse is found in Deuteronomy 6:2, *"Fear the Lord... keep all his ways... that your days may be prolonged."* Of course, if we revere and respect God then we will want to keep His commands. And there are many verses that tell us if we keep His commandments our days will be long on the earth. (See Deut. 4:40, 5:33, 11:9, 22:7 & 30:19-20.)

Allow me to comment on two of the above references. Deuteronomy 4:40 says, *"You shall keep therefore His statutes and His commandments, which I command you this day, that it may go well with you, and with your children after you, and that you may prolong your days upon the earth..."* This verse tells us that even the quality of our children's lives can be affected by our obedience or disobedience to God's commands. That should catch our attention!

I also really like what Deuteronomy 30:19-20 says. Verse 19 tells us to choose the life and blessing that God has provided for us. Then verse 20 tells us to love Him, obey His voice and cling to Him, and then it tells us why, *"...for He is your life and the length of your days."* Cling to Him—He is your lifeline!

Acts 17:28 says, *"In Him we live, and move, and have our being."* Let's face it, without God we are nothing, we have nothing and we can do nothing! He is our "everything!" And by giving Him first place in our lives we will live a long, prosperous life.

Let's go back to something we discussed earlier in this book. God's Word tells us to honor our father and mother so our days will be long on the earth. (See Ephesians 6:3, Exodus 20:12 & Deuteronomy 5:16.)

The Hebrew word for *honor* means *to be heavy or weighty.* You may have heard someone referring to a person of prominence or fame by saying something like, "That person throws his weight around" or, "That guy is a heavy hitter." Those phrases simply mean that some people look up to those who are *heavy* or *weighty.* They treat them with respect, defer to them and esteem them highly. Well, that's the way we're supposed to treat our parents!

Someone may say, "Well, my parents don't deserve honor because of the way they treated me." God didn't say to honor them if they are honorable. He said to honor them—period! So, guess what? Your obedience to God will cause your life to be blessed and extended. Therefore, He must be telling you to do it more for your benefit than for theirs!

Listen, if you are at odds with either of your parents, you had better make it right from your side, no matter what their actions are. You should love them, honor them and show respect to them—regardless of how they respond to or treat you! Your responsibility is to obey God no matter what others do. So, if you want to have a long, blessed life, then honor your parents. Amen!

Now look at Proverbs 28:16. It says, *"He that hates*

covetousness shall prolong his days." Another way to say it would be, *He who distances himself from greed and bribery will live a long life.* This is a warning to us, letting us know that we need to guard our hearts and minds with regard to money matters.

I've heard of family members who disowned each other because of disputes over inheritances. You had better watch out—you may be opening the door to a shortened life. What good is getting riches if you don't live long and have time to enjoy them? Jesus told us in Luke 12:15 to pay attention to and be on our guard against greed. He reminds us in that verse that our possessions are not what determine the quality of our lives. Proverbs 15:27 tells us that the person who is greedy of gain brings troubles to his own house. But Proverbs 1:19 is even more startling! In essence it says, *"If you become a greedy person, that greed will rob you of your own life."*

We've looked at numerous reasons why God's people are robbed of the long life (at least 120 years) that He has promised them. But let me reiterate something here. A major reason why God's people have not enjoyed the 120 years and longer is because of a lack of knowledge.

Hosea 4:6 says, *"My people are destroyed for a lack of*

knowledge." Isaiah 5:13 says, *"My people go into captivity because they have no knowledge."* Friends, listen, if Christians don't *know* God's will concerning long life they will never have the faith to receive it. Faith begins where the will of God is known. You cannot believe beyond actual knowledge.

If a child of God believes that 70, 80 or 90 years is long life then they'll get satisfied and go on to be with Jesus! But if our eyes are opened to the Word of Truth in this area, then we will realize that our latter years can be more fulfilling and rewarding than our earlier ones. We can still be strong and healthy physically, sharp mentally, blessed financially and full of the wisdom of God in our "old age" years. We can be like Moses when he was 120, *"...his eyes could still see clearly and his physical strength remained strong."* (Deuteronomy 34:7—My paraphrase.)

When God speaks of *long life* He is not only speaking of the length of our lives but also the quality of them. Listen, abundant life doesn't end when we get old! We are supposed to enjoy *more abundance* as we get older.

Chapter 8

Misconceptions

There is a phrase used in the Bible that has a tendency to make us think that "old" means frail, weak and decrepit. We see the phrase used when speaking about Abraham & Sarah, Zacharias & Elisabeth, as well as others. So let's look at the phrase. Genesis 18:11 says, *"Now Abraham and Sarah were old and well stricken in age; and it ceased to be with Sarah after the manner of women."* Also in Luke 1:7 it speaks about Zacharias and Elisabeth and says, *"...they were now well stricken in years."*

Notice the phrase "well stricken." When we think of the word *stricken* we usually associate it with someone who is suffering with sickness. And very often we associate the word with diseases such as strokes,

Alzheimer's, Parkinson's, arthritis, etc. All of these diseases tend to affect a larger percentage of older people than they do younger ones.

However, the words "well stricken" in Genesis 18:11 are not referring to being struck down with some "old peoples' disease." Actually, the words "well stricken" come from one Hebrew word which means *to enter in* or *come in*. In other words, Abraham and Sarah had *entered into* or *come into* old age. Of course, we know that Abraham and Sarah were in their nineties.

Likewise, the Greek word used for "well stricken" in Luke basically means the same thing as the Hebrew word. It means, *to go forward* or *go on*. In other words, Zacharias and Elisabeth had *gone forward* or *gone on* into years that were beyond their child-bearing years. So, in both cases, we can see that "well stricken" does not refer to being weak, feeble or in poor health.

Is Our Body Decaying?

Now let's look at another misconception. There is a verse in the New Testament that puzzled me for years. It seemed to contradict all of the verses that we've looked at so far. But years ago I learned a valuable truth, and that is: if a Scripture appears to contradict another one, then it simply means that I am not understanding or rightly dividing the Word of Truth. So, let's look at the verse to which I am referring. It is found in 2nd Corinthians 4:16.

> **For which cause we faint not; but though our outward man perish, yet the inward man is renewed day by day.**

I always thought the phrase *"though our outward man perish,"* meant that our bodies are wearing out and becoming weak and frail as we grow older.

However, in more recent times the Lord prompted me to study this verse *in context*. When I did I found out that Paul wasn't talking about "growing old" at all!

Of course, most Christians know God's Word was not spoken in chapters and verses. The chapters and verses were added for reference sake, so we could find things easily.

So, I went back to chapter 1 of 2nd Corinthians and read through chapter 5. In the first chapter Paul began talking about how he and Timothy were experiencing an abundance of evils and hardships, just like Jesus had faced. And in the 8th verse, he said their troubles were so severe they thought they were going to die.

Then, in the 4th chapter, Paul began deliberating along the same lines once again. In verses 8 and 9 he said they were *"troubled on every side... perplexed... persecuted."* In verses 10 and 11 he said they were close to death continually—so much so that he said in verse 12 that *"death works in us."* That simply means they were living in the face of death frequently. But, in the next 2 verses, Paul tells the Corinthians (and us) that he and Timothy were in faith about all the situations they were facing. In the next verse (verse 14) he said the same Spirit that raised Jesus from the dead would raise them up too, if necessary. Then he said, in verse 15, *"For all things are for your sakes"* and *"to the glory of God."* In other words, *we're going through all of this for you and God is going to be glorified abundantly!*

AFTER ALL THAT, Paul said in verse 16, *"For which cause we faint not; but though our outward man perish..."*

In other words, he was saying, "The cause of Christ is so strong in us that we are not going to weaken our stand. Even if we are destroyed physically, *we* will keep on living." Then he said in verses 17 and 18 that all the evils they were going through were pale in comparison to what God had in store for them.

But Paul didn't stop there. He continued in verse 1 of the next chapter. He said, *"If our earthly house* (our body) *were dissolved* (died), *we have a building of God, a house not made with hands, eternal in the heavens."*

In verse 16 of chapter 4 and verse 1 of chapter 5 Paul uses the words *"perish"* and *"dissolved"* respectively.

Paul wasn't talking about *our* bodies dissolving or perishing because of age. He was talking about *their* bodies dying or perishing because of being on the brink of death so many times.

In 2nd Corinthians 11:23-27, Paul lets us know about many of the life-threatening dangers he faced during his ministry. He said he was in prison frequently and faced death often, including being whipped five times, beaten with rods three times, stoned once and involved in three shipwrecks. In fact, when Paul was stoned in Lystra, he was dragged out of the city and left for dead! (See Acts 14:19-20.)

By studying the life and journeys of Paul you can see that he stared right into the face of death many times. And *that* is what Paul was talking about in 2nd

Corinthians 4:16. A good paraphrase of that verse would be *"even if they kill our bodies they won't be able to kill us. We (the real man on the inside) will keep living forever!"*

So, when he made that statement, he was not referring to our bodies falling apart and wearing out because they are growing older! In addition, all of the verses we have looked at in this book let us know that God wants us to be satisfied with a long life, full of vim, vigor and vitality!

A Healthy Body with Just Prayer & The Word?

We've already seen that living a life of disobedience and sin will shorten our lives. But there is something else that will shorten our lives, and that is *not taking care of our physical bodies.* Let me make it very simple: as important as it is to pray, read our Bibles and speak the Word, if we neglect our physical bodies we will not stay strong and healthy.

There are three things that we must give heed to with regard to our physical bodies. They are: diet, exercise and sleep.

Someone may think, "I don't believe it is important for

me to learn about those things."

Listen friend, the Bible tells us to *renew* our mind, not *remove* it! God gave us these brains to think with, and if we are wise we will do just what Proverbs 1:5 tells us, *"A wise man will hear and will increase learning."*

We can always learn more (in many different areas) no matter how much we already know. We can learn more about how to love our spouses, how to take care of our bodies, how to walk by faith and please God, how to live worry-free, how to become financially free and how to raise children, just to name a few. Besides, God has instructed us to do something with regard to our bodies. Look at Romans 12:1.

> **I beseech you therefore, brethren, by the mercies of God, that you present your bodies a living sacrifice, holy, acceptable unto God, *which is* your reasonable service.**

Young's Literal Translation reads, *"I call upon you, therefore, brethren, through the compassions of God, to present your bodies a sacrifice—living, sanctified, acceptable to God—your intelligent service."*

This verse doesn't tell us to present our *spirits*, it says to present our *bodies*. Look at the words used with regard to presenting our bodies—*living, sacrifice, holy* and *acceptable.* Those words indicate there are actions required on our part. There are things *we must do* to present our bodies to God. And this verse says that it is our *"reasonable service"* or, as Young's puts it, our *"intelligent service."* That means we have to use the brains God gave us in order to present our bodies correctly. Now look at 1st Corinthians 6:19-20.

> **What? Don't you know that your body is the temple of the Holy Ghost *which is* in you, which you have of God, and you are not your own? 20For you are bought with a price: therefore glorify God in your body, and in your spirit, which are God's.**

Verse 19 says your body is the temple of the Holy Ghost. Your body is a temple that has co-tenants, you and the Holy Ghost! And guess what else? You don't own that body you're living in. Verse 20 says that your body and your spirit belong to God. And it tells you to glorify God, not just in your spirit but also in *your body.*

Once again, this verse implies that there are actions

we have to take concerning our bodies that will bring glory to God.

Taking Care of Our Bodies

Let's now discuss the "natural side" of our longevity. Go back to the three things we listed that we must do with regard to our bodies. After all, we want to present them to God in a way that will glorify Him, don't we?

The three things I listed were diet, exercise and sleep. I could write a book on each of these subjects, though that is not the intent of this book. However, I will, as directed by the Holy Ghost, point out some essential truths in each of these areas.

Chapter 9

Proper Diet

Let's start out with the subject of *diet*. By using the word *diet* I simply mean *what we eat and drink*. There are multitudes of books on the market that deal with our diets, and some of them are good. However, even some of the good ones contain statements with which I disagree. That's because they say that you can't eat certain foods, yet in the Bible I see Jesus and His disciples eating them. So, I may adhere to 90% of a particular eating program, but the 10% that disagrees with Scripture, I ignore.

Let's take a look at a few New Testament Scriptures that deal with food. Like I indicated, I am not going to get into an in-depth teaching on these things, but I will point out some Scriptures that you can study for yourself. And remember this, the Bible teaches temperance. Temperance (self-control) is a key for every part of our lives, including the foods we eat!

Let's begin in Matthew 12:1. It says that Jesus and His disciples were walking along on the Sabbath day and the disciples began to pluck ears of corn from the cornstalks and eat them. Someone may say, "Corn is not good for you because it is just a carbohydrate." Listen, if eating corn was bad for you, Jesus would not have allowed His disciples to eat it. So, if it's good enough for Jesus, it's good enough for me!

Matthew 14:14-21 relates the story of Jesus and His disciples feeding 5,000 men plus women and children. Do you remember what they ate? They ate fish and whole-grain bread. And verse 19 says that Jesus blessed the food. So, these two foods must be among the ones that God can bless, which means they must be good for you! Selah.

In Matthew 15:32-38, we see the same two foods (fish and whole-grain bread) being eaten when Jesus fed 4,000 men, not counting the women and children. And once again Jesus thanked God for the food. So He must have had God's approval on it.

In Matthew 7:9-11 Jesus uses fish and bread as examples

when giving "good things" to our children, once more giving His approval for those foods.

In John 21:1-14 (after His resurrection) Jesus appears to his disciples for the third time. When they returned to the shore (from fishing) Jesus had a meal prepared for them. Guess what it was? That's right, bread and fish! (See verses 9 & 13.)

These two foods, fish and whole-grain bread, are definitely in God's book of approved cuisine!

Now look at Luke 15:11-32. It is the parable of the prodigal son. Before I teach from this parable, let me call your attention to something. When Jesus taught kingdom principles, He frequently used parables. (Parables use true-to-life examples to illustrate spiritual truths.) When Jesus used a parable to teach something good, He would use *good* things in the natural realm for the illustration. He never used ungodly or unclean things when illustrating a good kingdom principle. For example, when He taught about how to get the Word to produce fruit in our lives, He used a parable about sowing seed into the ground. When He taught about how the Kingdom of God can grow, He used a parable about a grain of mustard seed that grows into a huge tree and gives shelter. When He taught about Himself and His followers, He illustrated using sheep following a shepherd. All of these parables, and many more, use objects in this natural realm that are good. In other words, fruit, seed, harvest, trees for shelter, sheep and shepherds are not evil things, they are good things. So, once again, when Jesus used a parable to illustrate a good kingdom principle, He used natural things that were "good" for His illustration.

With that thought in mind let me ask you a question. In the parable of the prodigal son, what food did the prodigal son's father prepare in order to celebrate his son's return? Filet Mignon! ☺ Okay, that may be a "Larry Hutton Paraphrase," but look at verse 23. It says, *"Bring hither the fatted calf and kill it, and let us eat."*

The Greek word for *calf* means *a young cow, bullock or heifer.* That means it must be okay to eat meat from these animals.

In Proverbs 24:13, God said, *"eat honey because it is good."* Although in Proverbs 25:27, when talking about eating honey it says we shouldn't eat much of it. But a *little* honey is okay and obviously good in God's eyes.

Matthew 7:16-17 mentions grapes and figs as being

good fruit. In Mark 11:12-13 we see that Jesus was hungry and went to a fig tree to satisfy His appetite. This shows us that figs and grapes are also in God's book of approved foods.

In 1st Corinthians 9 Paul gives a discourse to the church about how we are to provide financially for our ministers so they don't have to work a secular job. And in verse 7, in his analogy, he points out that it's okay to eat the fruit we get from vineyards and the milk that comes from flocks (sheep).

Someone may ask, "Doesn't the Bible say we are to eat whatever is set before us?" Actually, there are verses which appear to express that idea, so let's look at them.

In Luke 10:7-8 it says, *"...eat such things as are set before you."* This was spoken by Jesus to the seventy disciples, whom He commissioned to go out and do the works He did. However, He only sent them *to the house of Israel*. That meant they were only visiting the Jewish people, who only set healthy food before them! So, this verse doesn't mean that *we* are supposed to eat everything that is set before us in today's society.

Now let's examine what is spoken in 1st Corinthians 10:27.

It says, *"...whatsoever is set before you eat..."* If you read this verse in context, you will find that this direction was given under a very specific set of circumstances.

Verse 25 says, *"Whatsoever is sold in the shambles, that eat, asking no question for conscience sake."* The word *shambles* referred to a place where meat and other articles of food were sold. So, this verse says that it was okay to eat any food that was sold at the market. But the following verses tell us why it was okay to eat them. Verse 26 says, *"For the earth is the Lord's, and the fullness thereof."*

Then verse 27 says, *"If any of them that believe not bid you to a feast, and you be disposed to go; whatsoever is set before you, eat, asking no question for conscience sake."*

Notice verses 25 and 27 end with the statement *"eat, asking no question for conscience sake."* But verse 27 reveals to us the occasion in which this applies. It says that if we are invited to eat with unbelievers and have a desire to go, then we can eat whatever is set before us without a guilty conscience because *"the earth is the Lord's and everything in it."* So, once again, this verse is not saying that we are supposed to eat everything that is offered on every occasion.

Now let's look at some more Scriptures with regard to what we eat.

Matthew 15:1-2 tells us that the Jewish leaders saw the disciples eating bread without washing their hands. According to the law that was unclean. But Jesus said in verse 11, it is not what goes into the mouth that defiles a man but what comes out of it. Then He gets more specific in verse 17, *"Do not ye yet understand, that whatsoever enters in at the mouth goes into the belly, and is cast out into the draught?"*

Jesus lets us know that whatever food we eat is going to be processed through the body and disposed of. Therefore, food does not defile the body. That doesn't mean that all foods are *good* for the body. God is just letting us know that foods won't corrupt us, but what comes out of our mouths can!

Water

Since we are discussing our diets, I feel that it is vitally important at this point to discuss the value of drinking enough water.

It's been said that many of the illnesses and pains that people experience in this country are a result of dehydration. By dehydration I mean not having sufficient amounts of water in the body.

Next to oxygen, water (which makes up over 70% of our body composition) is the most influential and vital component for the body to maintain health and prevent its deterioration.

Water helps remove the dangerous toxins that your body takes in from the air you breathe, the food you eat and the chemicals applied in the various products you use on your skin and hair. Water also plays a crucial role in regulating body temperature.

Our bodies are made up of almost 75% water. Approximately 85% of the brain, 80% of the blood and 70% of the muscle is water. And the lungs are nearly 90% water.

Since such a large percentage of our bodies is water, it obviously figures heavily in how our bodies function. We need lots of fresh water to stay healthy. Aside from aiding in digestion and absorption of food, water regulates body temperature and blood circulation, helps carry nutrients and oxygen to cells, and removes toxins and other wastes. This "body water" also cushions joints and protects tissues and organs, including the spinal cord, from shock and damage. Conversely, lack of water (dehydration) can be the root of many ailments.

Every process in our body occurs in a water medium. We can exist without food for 2 months or more, but we can only survive for a few days without water.

The digestive system depends heavily on the presence of generous amounts of water. The mucous that lines your stomach is 98% water. Without sufficient amounts of water, stomach acid will eat away at stomach cells and lead to decreased digestive efficiency. The kidneys are also involved in clearing out the body. The kidneys remove toxins and wastes from the body which must be dissolved in water. When there isn't sufficient water, those wastes are not effectively removed and become as poison to the body.

Also, without sufficient water the kidneys cannot work adequately, which affects some of the water going to the liver. One of the primary functions of the liver is to metabolize stored fat into energy for the body. If the liver needs to do some of the work of the kidneys, the liver cannot work as it should to metabolize fat. Therefore, more fat is stored in the body, increasing its weight and rendering the liver inefficient in using the fat as energy.

Water is what keeps the body's metabolism working at its optimum. Although water doesn't provide energy in the same way carbohydrates and fat do, it still plays an important role in energy transformation. Water is the medium in which all energy reactions occur. It helps move nutrients, hormones, antibodies and oxygen through the blood stream and lymphatic system. Water is the solvent of the body and regulates all functions, including the activity of everything it dissolves & circulates.

When the body is low on water it's like the engine of a car being low on oil. The lower the engine's oil supply the rougher it will run. And when the engine has depleted its supply of oil it will shut down. That's exactly what will happen to the body when it is low or depleted of its water supply!

Since our blood is 80% water, then a deficiency of water in the body will have an adverse effect on the brain. Although the brain is only 1/50th of the body's weight, it uses 1/20th of the blood supply. With dehydration, the level of energy generation in the brain is decreased. This definitely affects mental capabilities.

The body's actively growing blood cells in the bone marrow require water continually. And water is "king" when it comes to keeping things moving freely because it's a big part of the fluid that lubricates the body's bones and joints. The lubricating material of the joint, called synovial fluid, is almost all water, with some protein-carbohydrate molecules. Cartilage (at the end of bones and between vertebrae) is also very high in water content. When the body has plenty of water, both the lubricating fluid and the cartilage work together, causing everything to glide smoothly. If the cartilage is dehydrated, the rate of "abrasive" damage is increased, resulting in joint deterioration and increased pain.

Regarding the backbone, 75% of the upper body's weight is supported by the water volume that is stored in the spinal disc core. 25% is supported by the fibrous materials around the disc. The spinal joints are dependent on different hydraulic properties of water, which is stored in the disc core.

Many pains in the back and joints can be eliminated once the body becomes well hydrated *and* a regular exercise program is employed.

According to studies, water also plays a major part in weight loss. Dehydration leads to excess body fat, poor muscle tone and size, decreased digestive efficiency and organ function, increased toxicity, joint and muscle soreness—and, oddly enough, even water retention.

Since water contains no calories, it can serve as an appetite suppressant, and help the body metabolize stored fat. Water is also fat-free, cholesterol-free and low in sodium. When pertaining to losing weight, water may be the single most important nourishment you take in every day! Also, drinking more water helps to reduce water retention by stimulating your kidneys, and helps to keep muscles and skin toned.

Numerous studies have shown that chronic dehydration may cause certain problems for the body, including hypertension, depression, chronic fatigue, migraine headaches, asthma, blood clots, constipation, allergies, urinary tract infections, sore throats, dry cough, a hoarse voice, muscle cramps, joint pain and dry skin. Dehydration also causes stress which causes further dehydration.

"Brother Larry, how do I know if I'm dehydrated? And how much water do I need to drink daily?"

One way to check your body is to check your urine. It should be odorless and relatively clear. If it's golden or deep color with a strong odor, you're dehydrated and you need more water.

Every day your body loses large amounts of water. In fact, it can lose up to 2½ quarts of water, without excess perspiration or exercise. The body loses water via the skin by perspiration, kidneys by urine, lungs by exhaled water vapor, and intestine by feces. The body even loses water while you sleep.

Numerous health and nutrition experts recommend that you take your weight (in pounds), divide it by 2, and drink that many ounces of water each 24 hour period. In other words, if you weigh 128 pounds, you should drink 64 ounces (8 glasses) of water a day. If you weigh 192 pounds, you'll need 96 ounces (12 glasses) per day.

Drinking caffeinated coffee or tea will interfere with the ability to stay hydrated because they are both diuretics. Diuretics cause the kidneys to increase urine and salt excretion, thereby dehydrating the body further. (For each cup of coffee or glass of tea that you drink, add one 8 ounce glass of water to the above figures. Of course, it would be more beneficial to stay off caffeine altogether!)

Chapter 10

Exercise

Okay, we've been discussing the natural side of what we can do to glorify God in our bodies. The first thing was *proper diet*. The second one is *exercise*.

You may think that exercise is not important—but think again! Did you know that our bodies have approximately 650 muscles in them? Just what do you think God put them in the body for—simply to take up space? I think not!

Muscles have a variety of tasks. They hold the bones in the proper position. They keep the joints working properly. They help us push, pull, lift, squat, bend and climb, as well as many other things. And when our muscles are neglected, by not exercising them, they will become weak and unable to function the way God created them to.

Muscles are also major calorie and fat burners. Thus they aid us in keeping our bodies strong, fit and trim.

In order to keep our muscles working at their optimum potential, they have to be exercised. There must be some type of resistance training performed on a regular basis for our muscles to stay strong.

Most people are considerably active from their teenage years through their 30's. But by the time they enter their 40's and beyond they become so busy with work and other functions, that they no longer are getting the necessary activity to keep their muscles toned. That's when back problems, joint problems, injuries, high blood pressure, weight problems, etc. begin entering their lives.

These dilemmas can be avoided by incorporating physical exercise into their weekly schedule, and by not ignoring the other things we are discussing as well.

Other people grow up not being involved in any sports or strenuous physical activity; therefore, they don't see the importance of physical exercise. So their

650 muscles (and their other body parts that need the exercise) begin diminishing in strength and effectiveness, opening the door for many physical problems.

"Brother Larry, I just can't find the time to exercise."

Listen, finding time to exercise is like finding time to pray or study the Word of God. If you've been a Christian for very long you already know that you can't *find* time to study and pray, you have to *make* time. In other words, you have to plan your day *before* it arrives so that your schedule includes these things. You have to schedule a time to exercise. If you fail to plan—you plan to fail!

Our bodies need exercise. One very good reason is that exercise is a natural stress reliever. And relieving stress is essential in this fast-paced society. Stress is the cause of many illnesses, and for that reason alone *exercise is important!*

Exercise will also keep your heart strong. Remember, your heart is a muscle—it needs exercise.

When I speak of exercise I don't mean using your muscles a few times during the day at your job. I'm speaking of a 30 to 60 minute concentrated workout, with weight resistance, 3 times a week (every other day). Then, between those days, add 2 days of cardiovascular workouts, such as swimming, fast walking, jogging, etc. By cardiovascular, I mean an exercise that will keep your heart rate up for 30 minutes.

Another benefit of exercise is that it will help you sleep better. That is partly due to less stress.

"Well, Brother Larry, doesn't the Bible say that exercise does not profit us much?" No, as a matter of truth, that's not what the Bible says. Let's look at 1st Timothy 4:8.

> **For bodily exercise profits little but godliness is profitable unto all things, having promise of the life that now is, and of that which is to come.**

The word *little* means *for a little while* or *a short amount of time,* making reference to a specific time period. The rest of the verse lets us know *what time period* it is referring to. It goes on to say that godliness is profitable in *"the life that now is"* but, unlike exercise, that promise extends to our next life as well. So, the *little while,* with regard to physical exercise, is referring to *"the life that now is."* In other words, both exercise and godliness have a promise for this life, but godliness also has a promise *"of the life... which is to come."*

The *"life that now is"* refers to the 120 (or more) years that we can live in this physical body. And when you compare our 120+ years here on the earth to our never-ending life in the hereafter, you would probably say the same thing as the Apostle James, *"What is your life? It is even a vapor that appears for a little time and then vanishes away."* (James 4:14)

The 120+ years that we can live in our mortal bodies is like a vapor, when compared to the time we will live in our immortal bodies. Our life span here on the earth is a *short amount of time,* and during that period of time bodily exercise will benefit us.

Notice again the verse in 1st Timothy 4:8. It says that bodily exercise and godliness have a *"promise for this life."* The word *promise* in this verse means *a promised good or blessing.* Of course, we know that godliness will cause good things and blessings to come our way, but so will exercise!

God says that physical exercise will be rewarded in this life. And part of that reward is to be strong and fit in our physical bodies, even in our "old age" years.

So, that verse in Timothy isn't saying that we get very little profit from exercising. On the contrary, it is letting us know that we will benefit from exercise in this present life.

Another way to look at the "little while" with regard to exercise is the fact that you can't just exercise one time in this life and expect the benefit to last your whole lifetime.

If you have ever started an exercise program and then quit for a time, you realized that you only benefited from that exercise "for a little while."

That's why we have to make exercise a lifestyle, not just something we do until we get the weight off or feel better. We must keep doing it in this present life if we want the rewards it will bring us.

Besides, this isn't just about us keeping our bodies in shape *for us,* but it's about *glorifying God in our bodies!*

Chapter 11

Sleep

Now let's discuss the 3rd thing that we need to do to keep our bodies in good physical shape, so we can glorify God in them—Sleep!

I don't know about you, but I am looking forward, with eagerness, to that wonderful day when we get our glorified bodies. Do you want to know one reason why? Because we won't have to waste time sleeping anymore!

However, in this life sleep is important. Look at Mark 4:35-41. Jesus and His disciples are on a ship going across the sea to the country of the Gadarenes. Verse 38 says that Jesus was asleep on a pillow. And, He was *sound asleep*, so much so that neither the storm nor the water filling up the ship could wake Him! Listen friends, if Jesus (the only human that never sinned) needed sleep—then so do we!

Now look at Psalm 4:8. It says, *"I will both lay me down in peace, and sleep: for you LORD make me dwell in safety."*

The New Jerusalem Bible says, *"In peace I lie down and at once fall asleep, for it is you and none other, Yahweh, who make me rest secure."*

(My paraphrase) *When I lay down to sleep, I do so in peace, because you, Lord, will keep me safe and secure.*

This verse not only lets us know that we need sleep, but also that our sleep is supposed to be a tranquil time. Our bodies need rest in order to stay strong. In fact, many restoration processes take place in our bodies when we are sleeping properly.

Look at Psalm 127:2. *"It is vain for you to rise up early, to sit up late, to eat the bread of sorrows: for so he gives his beloved sleep."*

(My paraphrase) *It is unproductive to let hurt feelings, sorrows or hardships rob you of sleep by keeping you awake at night or awakening you too early in the morning.*

For God has promised you the sleep you need.

Let's look at one more Scripture regarding sleep. Proverbs 3:24 says, *"When you lie down, you shall not be afraid: yes, you shall lie down, and your sleep shall be sweet."*

The New Living Translation says, *"You can lie down without fear and enjoy pleasant dreams."*

Let me quote Proverbs 3:24-26 from the Message Bible. It is really good.

> **You'll take afternoon naps without a worry. You'll enjoy a good night's sleep. No need to panic over alarms or surprises, or predictions that doomsday's just around the corner. Because GOD will be right there with you; He'll keep you safe and sound.**

What kind of sleep does God want us to have? Sweet, pleasant sleep, free from fear and worries! Stand on God's Word. He has already promised you sleep, so use your faith and possess it!

Obviously, for God to say these things, sleep must play an important role in our lives.

Sleep, like diet and exercise, is important for our minds and bodies to function normally. Scientists say that the body is as active during sleep as it is when we're awake.

Researchers have shown that while we sleep we are cycling through different states of consciousness, moving in and out of dream states. While this is happening our bodies are actively restoring vital chemical balances—all in preparation for a new day.

Studies suggest that it is during "deep sleep" (the kind God wants to bless us with) the body is able to restore organs, bones and tissue, replenish immune cells and circulate a rejuvenating supply of growth hormone.

Research has also revealed that sleep disorders can shorten lives, weaken the immune system, as well as bones and joints, and contribute to heart attacks, strokes, high blood pressure, decreased productivity, failure on the job and auto accidents.

Tests have shown that there are numerous reasons for the inability to sleep well. Included in the list are poor diet, lack of exercise, stress and accumulation of toxins in the body (from the environment, food, drugs and other sources).

Listen, if we are eating right, exercising and staying in peace then we can use our faith for God to bless our sleep. Why? Because He said He would! And since we need good sleep to be healthy and strong physically and mentally, then let's not settle for anything less than God's best! Amen!

Chapter 12

Take Control of Your Body

Listen, we can train our bodies to do whatever we want them to do! The Apostle Paul said, *"I keep under my body, and bring it into subjection."* (1st Corinthians 9:27) The New Living Translation says, *"I discipline my body like an athlete, training it to do what it should."*

We can make our bodies do whatever we want. But our inner man (the spirit) has to be stronger than the outer man (the body). That's why God's Word must be daily bread. It is the fuel for the spirit man just like food is fuel for the body.

When *we* are in control of our bodies *we* will feed them the foods they need, and not feed them *more* than they need. If we allow our bodies to eat more than they should, they will become overweight. This will definitely not glorify God in our bodies. This is something we should give heed to because God dealt with it in Proverbs 23:2. It says, *"And put a knife to thy throat, if thou be a man given to appetite."*

This verse indicates that our bodies may want to eat more than they need. And the phrase *"put a knife to your throat"* simply means, don't allow your body to eat more than it needs. You must control your body; don't let it control you.

Furthermore, eating does not satisfy the spirit or soul of man, it only satisfies the body. Ecclesiastes 6:7 tells us that we work to put food on the table, yet our souls are not satisfied.

When people go on eating binges, they are trying to satisfy a spiritual problem with natural means. You, the spirit man, must learn to control your body; otherwise you'll be a mess.

Look at Proverbs 25:28. It says, *"He that has no rule over his own spirit is like a city that is broken down, and without walls."*

In other words, if you allow yourself to be controlled by *your emotions,* your life will be a mess with no protection. And if your emotions are out of control, your body will be too! Take charge of your emotions and your body!

<u>Warning</u>!

Now, let me share one more thing with regard to the things we put in our bodies. Back in Jesus' day there were no processed foods. Everything was natural with no preservatives, additives, chemicals, dyes, etc. We could say that everything was "health food." Yet there was still *"every manner of sickness and every manner of disease among the people."* (See Matthew 4:23.) So, if health food alone would keep you healthy, there would have been no sick people for Jesus to heal!

The Lord told me one time not to put my faith in the foods I eat to keep me healthy, but to keep my faith in Him. (Note: Jesus wasn't telling me not to eat healthy foods; He was just reminding me of where to keep my trust.)

You see, there are many other things besides eating poorly that will open the door to sickness and disease. For example, worry, stress, strife, offenses and unforgiveness can bring all kinds of physical problems our way—no matter how well we eat!

Furthermore, we must remember there is a thief out there (the devil, evil one, wicked one, destroyer, enemy, deceiver, devourer, satan and father of lies) who will try to steal, kill and destroy us if we allow him to. But when we are submitted to God, then we can resist the devil (and all his attacks) and he will flee every time!

(Now, just in case there is someone who is reading this book and thinking that I made a mistake in not capitalizing the words *devil* or *satan*, HE IS A DEFEATED FOE AND I REFUSE TO GIVE HIM ANY HONOR! Jesus whipped, stripped and made a spectacle of him and placed him under my feet—a place of dishonor! And, as far as I'm concerned, that's where he will stay!) AMEN!

Chapter 13

Meditations & Confessions

Here are some more Scriptures to meditate on, fill your heart with and speak out loud daily. They will help you live a long life—in length and quality! After you read each Scripture, I will give you a confession of faith. Be bold as you speak the Word. Your declaration of truth will change the facts! It will change your life forever!

Psalm 103:2-5 *Bless the LORD, O my soul, and forget not all his benefits:* *³Who forgives all your iniquities; who heals all your diseases;* *⁴Who redeems your life from destruction; who crowns you with loving kindness and tender mercies;* *⁵Who satisfies your mouth with good things; so that your youth is renewed like the eagle's.*

DECLARE IT! Father God, you are my Lord and I bless you, praise you and adore you. And I thank you for all your benefits. I will not forget them. Lord, you forgive me of all my guilt, sin and shame. You heal me of every sickness and disease. You redeem me from destruction. You surround me with your goodness, kindness and faithfulness, and also with your compassion and mercy. You satisfy my mouth with good things. Therefore, my youth is renewed and I stay strong like an eagle, including my eyesight!

Proverbs 4:20-22 *My son, attend to my words; incline your ear unto my sayings. [21]Let them not depart from your eyes; keep them in the midst of your heart. [22]For they are life unto those that find them, and health* (strength, medicine) *to all their flesh.*

DECLARE IT! Dear God, I give your Words top priority in my life. I choose daily to hear what you have to say. I keep my eyes fixed on your Words and I keep my heart full of them. Your Words are my lifeline! They fill every part of my life with your life. That includes my body. Your words bring a cure, health, strength and medicine to every fiber and cell of my flesh. Therefore, my body is full of your strength, health and life.

Romans 8:11 *If the Spirit of him that raised up Jesus from the dead dwells in you, he that raised up Christ from the dead shall also quicken your mortal bodies by his Spirit that dwells in you.*

<u>DECLARE IT</u>! The same Spirit that raised Jesus from the dead lives in me. Holy Spirit, you quicken my mortal body. My physical body is infused with divine life. Every cell of my body is filled with the life of God. I have no cancer cells in my body because the life of God is quickening every cell of my body. My body is full of God's life and health, from the top of my head to the soles of my feet!

Deuteronomy 34:7 *And Moses was an hundred and twenty years old when he died: his eye was not dim, nor his natural force abated.*

<u>DECLARE IT</u>! Dear God, you are no respecter of persons. You promised me at least 120 years. When Moses was 120 years old he was still physically strong and had good eyesight. Therefore, I will live longer than 120 years, and I will be healthy and strong with good eyesight until the day I die.

Psalm 91:1-16 (The Good News Translation) *Whoever goes to the LORD for safety, whoever remains under the protection of the Almighty, ²can say to him, "You are my*

defender and protector. You are my God; in you I trust."
*³He will keep you safe from all hidden dangers and from all
deadly diseases. ⁴He will cover you with his wings; you
will be safe in his care; his faithfulness will protect and
defend you. ⁵You need not fear any dangers at night or
sudden attacks during the day ⁶or the plagues that strike in
the dark or the evils that kill in daylight. ⁷A thousand may
fall dead beside you, ten thousand all round you, but you
will not be harmed. ⁸You will look and see how the wicked
are punished. ⁹You have made the LORD your defender, the
Most High your protector, ¹⁰and so no disaster will strike
you, no violence will come near your home. ¹¹God will put
his angels in charge of you to protect you wherever you go.
¹²They will hold you up with their hands to keep you from
hurting your feet on the stones. ¹³You will trample down
lions and snakes, fierce lions and poisonous snakes. ¹⁴God
says, "I will save those who love me and will protect those
who acknowledge me as LORD. ¹⁵When they call to me, I
will answer them; when they are in trouble, I will be with
them. I will rescue them and honor them. ¹⁶I will reward
them with long life; I will save them."*

DECLARE IT! Heavenly Father, I am so glad that you
dwell in me and that I dwell in you. You are my
defender and my protector. I trust in you—you
alone. Father, you keep me safe from all hidden
dangers and deadly diseases. You keep me covered
and safe. Your faithfulness will protect and defend

me. I don't fear anything! Tens of thousands may fall all around me, but I will not be harmed. Lord, I have made you my defender and protector, therefore no disaster will strike me and no violence will come near my home. God, you have put your angels in charge of me. They are protecting me wherever I go. They will hold me in their hands so that no part of me will be hurt. I trample down every type of danger and evil that comes my way. God, I love you and acknowledge you, so you save me and protect me. When I call upon you, you answer me. You are with me whenever I face trouble. You rescue me and honor me. Lord God, you reward me with long life. You continually show me your salvation—your welfare, prosperity and deliverance!

Proverbs 3:1-2 *My son, forget not my law; but let your heart keep my commandments: ²For length of days, and long life, and peace, shall they add to you.*

DECLARE IT! Father God, I will not forget your law of love nor will I forget your Words. I love you with all my heart, soul, mind and all my strength. And I love my neighbor (that's everyone else) and care for them with the same preferential treatment I give myself. I also keep your Words in my heart and act upon them. I obey your Word and that causes length of days, long life and peace to be added to me.

1 Peter 3:10 *For he that will love life, and see good days, let him refrain his tongue from evil, and his lips that they speak no guile.*

DECLARE IT! Lord God, I want to enjoy my life and see it filled with good things. Therefore, I do not allow my tongue to speak anything that is troublesome or destructive. And no lies or deceiving words will come out of my mouth.

Proverbs 3:13, 16 *Happy is the man who finds wisdom and the man who gets understanding. ¹⁶Length of days is in her right hand; and in her left hand riches and honor.*

DECLARE IT! I discover and increase in wisdom constantly. I am in Christ and His wisdom is in me. I continually acquire understanding by drawing it out of God's Word and listening to the Holy Spirit. Therefore, wisdom gives me a long, good life, and fills it with riches and honor. I am healthy, wealthy and wise!

Conclusion

What To Do Now

"Brother Larry, this is awesome! Now I know that God wants to satisfy me with long life. That is, He wants me to live longer than 120 years and be healthy and strong the whole time. But this is all so new to me. My heart is leaping for joy at the truth of God's Word, but thoughts of doubt and unbelief are coming at me like machine-gun bullets! So, what is my next step? What do I need to do to make sure that I fulfill God's plan for my life?"

The truth is, we have to get our hearts and minds so full of God's Word that it becomes all that we think and speak. When we hear and speak God's Word continually, it becomes easy to believe God for anything! In fact, we can be *strong in faith* just like Abraham. Romans 4:21 says he was *"strong in faith"* and *"fully persuaded"* that God would do everything that

He promised. Do you know how God got Abraham to that point? He changed his name! That's right. The only way God could make Abraham *the father of many nations* was to change what Abraham believed. In order to do that, God had to change what Abraham thought and spoke about himself. So God changed Abraham's name to "Father of many nations." Every time Abraham spoke his name, heard his name spoken, or thought about his name, his faith grew stronger. Likewise, our faith can grow stronger if we change what we believe and speak.

Galatians 3:9 says, *"They which are of faith are blessed with faithful Abraham."* We can operate in the same faith as Abraham. But we must do the same thing that Abraham did—believe and speak only what God says. That's also the same thing God told Joshua to do in Joshua 1:8.

> **This book of the law** [the Word of God] **shall not depart out of your mouth. But you shall meditate therein day and night, that you may observe to do according to all that is written in it. For then you shall make your way prosperous, and then you shall have good success.**

Let me paraphrase that for you. *You must relentlessly speak God's Word. Think about it continually whenever you're awake so that you do everything it says. Then every area of your life will prosper. You will have insight into everything you do. You will act prudently and wisely; thus, you will enjoy good success!*

As a child of God you should want His will to be accomplished in your life. Well, it's His will to satisfy you with long life. Begin to implement God's Word in this area. And then put God first in every area of your life. Do you remember how strong Caleb was when he was 85? Well, Numbers 14:24 tells us why. In that verse God declares, *"My servant Caleb... has followed me fully. Him will I bring into the land."* You must follow God fully. Follow his Word. It gives instructions concerning your body, your mind, your food, your actions, your marriage, your friendships, your children, your thoughts, your money, and anything else you can think of. Following Him fully will cause you to achieve a long life, filled with God's love, joy, peace, health and prosperity!

May your latter days be your best!

Larry ☺

I Have Finished This Book — Now What?

For further feeding, more revelation and increased strength we offer three other resources. Our book, *"Internal Affairs"* will help you gain more understanding about using your faith to overcome the problems of life. If you don't overcome them, they will overcome you, and that will not aid you in living a long, healthy life! Our Scripture tape *"Power Up"* will empower you on a daily basis to live victoriously. It is daily bread that is full of faith, victory and power, and will give you the energy and strength that you need to be a winner every day. Finally, we strongly recommend our Scripture tapes *"Wisdom Scriptures."* It has been said that a proverb a day will keep the doctor away. Well, I don't know about that, but I do know that God said, *"Wisdom is the principal thing; therefore get wisdom.* (Proverbs 4:7) *"Wisdom Scriptures"* is our 4-tape or CD collection of the entire book of Proverbs. It will fill your life with wisdom and open the doorway for all of God's blessings to come into your life. All of our Scripture tapes (which have no preaching, just Scriptures being quoted from multiple translations over a musical background) come in either CD or cassette, and are available through our website at: www.lhm.net .

To Contact
Larry Hutton Ministries
Write:

Larry Hutton Ministries
P.O. Box 822
Broken Arrow, OK 74013-0822

Or use one of the following methods:

Phone: (918) 259-3077
Fax: (918) 259-3158
E-mail: admin@lhm.net
Website: www.lhm.net

*Please include your prayer requests
and comments when you contact us.*

VERY IMPORTANT MESSAGE

God wants a personal relationship with every person in the world, including you! God is not mad at you, and He is not counting up all of your sins and holding them against you. He sent Jesus Christ to shed His blood, die on the cross and then be raised from the dead. And He did all that just so that you can be freed from the bondage of sin and enter into eternal life with a loving Heavenly Father.

If you have never accepted Jesus Christ as your personal Lord and Savior, it is very simple to do. The Bible states in Romans 10:13, *"Whosoever calls on the name of the Lord shall be saved."* Since it says, *"Whosoever"* then your name is in the Bible! Verses 9 and 10 tell us how easy it is to receive salvation (eternal life). They tell us that if we will say with our mouths that Jesus is our Lord, and believe in our hearts that God raised Him from the dead, we *"shall be saved."* It is that easy!

If you have never accepted Jesus as your Lord and Savior, then do it today! Say the following prayer out loud—right now:

Dear God, I want to be part of your family. You said in your Holy Word that if I would acknowledge that you raised Jesus from the dead, and that I accept Him as my personal Lord and Savior, I would be saved. So God, I now say that I believe you raised Jesus from the dead and that He is alive and well. I accept Him now as my personal Lord and Savior. I accept my salvation from all sin right now. I am now saved. Jesus is my Lord and Savior. Thank you, God, for forgiving me, saving me and giving me eternal life. Amen!

If you just prayed this prayer for the first time, I welcome you to the family of God! According to the Bible, in John 3:3-6, you are now born-again. Now it is very important, as a newborn child of God, that you get fed the milk of God's Word so that you can grow up in God and become a mature Christian.

If you will take the time to write, fax or e-mail us at the addresses listed on page 126, we would love to send you some free literature to help you in your new walk with the Lord. We will also be more than happy to help you find a good church that preaches the Word of God—not the traditions of men. This is vitally important for your future success in God.

Finally, come see us sometime, we would love to meet you! Our itinerary is included in our free magazine *The Force of Faith,* as well as on our website.

Other Materials
By
Force of Faith Publications

Books

➢ God, the Gold, and the Glory:
   Glorifying God through Personal Increase

➢ Internal Affairs:
   Emotional Stability in an Unstable World

Teaching Tapes - Series

➢ The Goodness of God
➢ Healing School
➢ Jesus the Healer
➢ Healing Made Easy
➢ How to Change Your Circumstances
➢ The Rich Young Ruler:
   The Story You've Never Heard
➢ Final Countdown:
   Your Launching Pad to Financial Freedom
➢ Heavyweight Champion of the World:
   Overcoming the Problems of Life
➢ Roof Rippin' Power:
   Activating God's Power for the Miraculous

Teaching Tapes - Singles

- Faith to be Healed (How to Keep Your Healing)
- No More Blue Mondays
- God's Healing Medicine
- Questions and Answers on Healing
- Redeemed From Sickness
- Don't Quit: Your Miracle is Here!
- Working for a Living: It's a Trap!

Scripture Tapes

- Heaven's Health Food:
  Healing and Health Scriptures
- Heaven's Wealth Food:
  Prosperity and Wealth Scriptures
- Power Up:
  Victorious Living Scriptures
- Wisdom Scriptures:
  All of Proverbs (a 4-volume set)

Music

- The Greatest Gift (Larry's Singing Album)
- Peace Be Still (Instrumental: Piano & Strings)
- Perfect Peace (Instrumental: Piano only)

ABOUT THE AUTHOR

LARRY HUTTON is a dynamic teacher and preacher for the body of Christ today! He teaches and preaches with a prophetic voice that is changing the lives of multitudes.

In 1980, God spoke to Larry in an audible voice and said, "Keep it simple, my Word is simple!" With that mandate from heaven, Larry has become widely acclaimed for the clarity and simplicity with which he teaches God's Word. He believes that the Bible is for us today and that we ought to be able to understand what it is saying so we can apply it and reach our God-given potential. He also believes that we don't have to wait until we get to the "sweet by and by" to enjoy God's blessings. Larry emphasizes that God wants us to enjoy His blessings in the "sweet here and now!" Through plain and practical teaching, Larry shows us what those blessings are, as well as how to receive and enjoy them.

Larry is nationally and internationally known as a speaker, TV host, author, singer and songwriter. He has become a popular guest speaker at church meetings, seminars, campmeetings and on Christian television. His teachings about divine healing, prosperity and victorious Christian living have to the truth that <u>we</u> have a major role in determining the length of our lives.

Additional copies of this book are available from
LARRY HUTTON MINISTRIES, INC.

FORCE OF FAITH PUBLICATIONS
Broken Arrow, OK 74012